I Look Up to Lead

(A Leadership Devotional)

CHARI DELA CRUZ

© 2016 by Chari Dela Cruz. All rights reserved.

No part of this publication may be reproduced, stored in a retrieval system, or transmitted in any form by any means, electronic, mechanical, photocopy, recording, or otherwise, without the permission of the publisher, except as provided for by the USA copyright law.

Author's Note: While this book's utmost desire is to inspire its readers to be guided by the Holy Spirit as leaders to pursue their first step, or to some, a deeper intimacy in their walk with the Lord, it is my prayer that you will not try to misuse the content of this book and make it your own.

ISBN-13: **978-1537540856**
ISBN-10: **1537540858**

First printing 2016
Printed in the United States of America

Unless otherwise indicated, Scripture quotations are from ESV® Bible (*The Holy Bible, English Standard Version®*)

DEDICATION

To
Artaj Dela Cruz
My first born, whom I believe is destined to be a leader for God

Table of Contents

DEDICATION	3
FOREWORD	6
INTRODUCTION	13
First Thing's First	15
Finding the strength	19
Audience of One	23
Visit Me Today	27
Perseverance	31
Letting Go	35
Working with Excellence	39
When I fail	43
New Beginnings	48
Prayer before I Coach	53
Inspiration	58
Thank You when my heart says, No Thank You.	62
Humility	67

FOREWORD

"Everyone wins when a leader gets better."

This is a common statement you'll hear from Bill Hybels, the person behind the Global Leadership Summit. As a yearly leadership conference touching hundreds of thousands of people all over the globe, the Summit provides both church and business leaders with current thinking and leadership insights from some of the best and brightest leaders today. It was in this setting that Chari felt God nudge her to put to words her experiences in leadership.

I love stories that emerge this way. Not from an academic classroom, but from the day-to-day challenges of leadership. From the inspiration of hearing others do it well. From the response to God's movement in our lives. As one of the pastors of the church Chari and her family attend, I wish we had more of these stories emerge from our community. Maybe this devotional will be the catalyst for you to be the next one.

I pray this devotional encourages your leadership as you begin each new week. The leader knows new challenges will arise but cannot foresee them in advance. By starting our week grounded in prayer and God's Word, we prepare ourselves for all that comes. For all the problems that need a solution and the people who need to be encouraged. For a world that needs change.

Chari Dela Cruz models a leader continually in the process of getting better. The result is that we win by reading what she writes in these pages. But don't let it stop there. As you get better as a leader, you allow all those who interact with you to win too.

Jeremy Jernigan
Executive Pastor at Central Christian Church, author of Redeeming Pleasure

23 Whatever you do, work heartily, as for the Lord and not for men,
Colossians 3:23

INTRODUCTION

I've come to realize that to live out the path that the Lord has called us to do, is not going to be a matter of a one-time big time event or phenomenon that will magically appear when we wake up. This book is an attempt to fulfill a calling that I believe the Lord has impressed in my heart.

I started leading people in 2005. I was recently promoted as a Team Leader in a call center in the Philippines for one of the best Business Process Outsourcers in our country at that time. I wasn't interviewed for that since I had just been recently interviewed six months ago for the same role which I lost to a non-college degree holder. I was so bitter about it and kept telling myself that diplomas don't really matter. After a few months, I got the news that I had been promoted for another account.

This is my first experience of God's Sovereignty and His plan is far greater than what we can hope for or imagine (Ephesians 3:20). After a few months of bitterness for not being accepted for the job I applied for, and then eventually getting promoted for another account, the first one was dissolved and had to close.

Fast forward to a decade. I write this book as a reminder of the many hurts that I could have avoided had I looked to my good, good Father. Those several days of sleepless nights and useless tears. Had I anchored myself to His Word and promises, He is the only comfort that I need. The joy that I only long for. He is not only the maker of any CEO I worked for, but King of kings, and Lord of lords.

It is my deepest prayer that through this book, you will allow the Lord to speak to your heart as a leader, and cast out all your anxieties and fears to Him.

I recommend that we surrender each first working day of the week to our Father who has prepared all the good things we ought to do in advance (Ephesians 2:10). It is designed to be read for the whole quarter of a year and create a habit and longing for how the Lord will transform your lives. If you are not a believer or have only started your journey in faith, I pray that this book will be a start of a life transforming leadership journey for you.

> 10 fear not, for I am with you;
>
> be not dismayed, for I am your God;
>
> I will strengthen you, I will help you,
>
> I will uphold you with my righteous right hand.
>
> Isaiah 41:10 (ESV)

First Thing's First

Leadership is not an easy task. The burden is far greater if we do not have a compass to guide us on our day to day struggles. I pray that through "prayer and supplication, with thanksgiving, our requests be made known to the Lord, and that peace which transcends all understanding be with us, in Christ Jesus" (Philippians 4:6-7).

I usually dread Mondays, but as a leader, it is such a privilege to let God be the anchor of our week and allow Him to bless us, teach us, and mold us throughout our week. Many leaders, including our teams, would rather spend their time with their families or maybe just lay in bed. It is not because we are good or we are smart enough to create our own paths and that is why we are the boss, but many times we fail to realize that all work is a gift from God. (Ecclesiastes 5:19)

I pray that you will start each week with a surrendered heart. True to servant leadership, we surrender to our master our power, our heart, and our positions.

God bless you!

Father, My Lord,

You set my feet on the ground today to be where I am.
Right here, right now.
Though with a heavy heart, and aching back, Here I am
May the meditations of my heart be hinged on your promises today.
Truly, I did not deserve the sunlight nor the melodic rustling of the trees today.
But you did it out of the infinite goodness of Your heart.
Thank you.
For new mercies, new grace, and new hope that I do not deserve.
As I start a new week, may I lift my hands to you, in sincere belief that I am here not because of my own intelligence nor strength, but because of the unique calling of leadership.
You called me, by my name, and have set out to make a difference in their (can also place the names of your direct reports) lives.
And in so doing, may they see who my Father is.
I need you. Because I am foolish and always forget that I can't do it alone.
Please hold my hand throughout this week. Go ahead of me and set my path.
Let no selfish desire get in the way of loving each of the sheep you have given me.

In your most beautiful name,
Amen.

9 For in him the whole fullness of deity dwells bodily,
10 and you have been filled in him, who is the head of all rule and authority.
Colossians 2:9-10

Week 1 Leadership Challenge:

What is it the first thing you can do this week that will bring honor to God?

Finding the strength

Many times in a leader's life, we have a nudging feeling of just giving up. We have doubts about our calling and wallow in an increasing feeling of depleting strength. This is most especially true when we hear a discouraging word from others. We immediately see how lacking we are and forget our true identity in Christ.

We are fearfully and wonderfully made! No amount of negative news can withstand the love of our Father to us!

When we think we will not be able to finish the race, and we are just at the end of our patience or frustration, when no one seems to understand, when we feel like we have exhausted all our reserved strength, may this prayer help us reignite our passions as we hold on to our one true source of strength, our Jesus.

Lord, I praise You!

for the gift of leadership
to affect the life of another with my own life.
I pray that all who are burdened by this role
be so humbled by the enormous responsibility
and learn that through Your strength alone can we be truly
anointed and blessed.

Use my hands as You would be here on earth
and fill my mind with Your knowledge and wisdom
that I may discern Your will for your people.

I surrender to you all that wishes me harm.
I rest in the truth that though the enemy will try to deceive
me, and lure me of the esteem offered by this world,
You have fought the battle for me.

I am tired by the demands of this world. Renew my strength.
You have said in Your word that in my weakness, Your
strength is made perfect.

Give me Your patience, Your love, Your wisdom.
May I look to You for assurance that this path You have
called me to be in is truly Your calling for me.

I pray that that throughout this week, with my aching soul,
You will remind what great love You have for me.
And in this overflowing love, through Your grace and the
Holy Spirit, I may pass on to Your people.

In Your most beautiful name,
Amen.

20 For the Father loves the Son and shows him all that he himself is doing.
And greater works than these will he show him, so that you may marvel.
John 5:20

Week 2 Leadership Challenge:

What do you want to give up this week but with God's grace will keep pressing on even for just another week?

Audience of One

One of the most difficult temptations a leader has to overcome is to find security in the affirmation of their bosses or direct reports. I remember the nights where I sneak in short naps throughout the night with my laptop on my chest to ensure that I respond to the email right away whenever my client sends a note out. Every good job is like getting a trophy, and every escalation feels like I and my team will lose our jobs.

The leadership drug, as others call it, is so addictive. It gives such a high when many sleepless nights result in improvements to Key Performance Indicators or dollar profit. Eventually, when things turn around, as it will very quickly, we are back to restlessness, fire-fighting and the vicious cycle of busyness. Our souls die, and our strength fails.

May this prayer remind all of us that the One who gave us this gift, is the only One that matters.

Oh, how I pray that we hunger and wait expectantly for the applause of our One God.

Dear Lord,

As we go about this week,
remind us that it's a great privilege to represent You to Your people.
Strengthen us to see beyond the surface of busyness and choose gratitude over grumbling.
Let all criticisms be carefully considered for the sole purpose of molding our characters.

With humility, give us a teachable heart.
May we serve with joy in the shadow of your glory.
May we generously spend time with the unnoticed and never count any credit.
Because truly, the greatest reward is not in any applause of men but of You.

Guard our hearts from hunger for affirmation from men.
Do not let the enemy deceive us that overwhelming due dates and targets means we are better than others, and only we can solve the problems.

Oh, shut the lie of the enemy that our significance is in our back to back meetings.

Instead, allow us to ponder as we see the sparrow, who never dies of hunger because of your providence. How much more are we, as your children? (Matt 6:26)
Ignite our hearts to pant only to Your applause, as a deer pants for water.

Let the one smile we all look forward to, be in heaven. Jesus, please, help us lead with an audience of One.

In Your most powerful name, I pray,
Amen.

23 Whatever you do, work heartily, as for the Lord and not for men,
24 knowing that from the Lord you will receive the inheritance as your reward. You are serving the Lord Christ.
Colossians 3:23-24 (ESV)

Week 3 Leadership Challenge:

How can we change our desire to please others this week, and instead please God?

Visit Me Today

Maybe you will have a business review this week, a very important meeting, or a performance review. Maybe a big presentation for which you have prepared all of the last week kept you up most nights. Your adrenaline might be pumped with caffeine and you just feel so important that no one can bother you.

Whatever it is you think is important right now, may you be reminded of the eternal perspective we have in Christ. I have not met anyone in his deathbed wishing he had one more hour to prepare for that crucial interview or whatever meeting it is.

I pray that even before you start this week, may this prayer hold you back and remember your identity in Christ. May we be so careful not to strike our foot on a stone of regret for not gaining wisdom that only the Lord provides.

Seek for His presence and feel it as you stand still in the eye of this storm that you are in.

My Jesus,

I pray for an open heart and mind that I may see Your presence through others.
May every customer or colleague, or team member be treated as you, Jesus.
You taught me that listening is loving.
I want to see Your love and give Your love with the act of listening and hearing.
Let others to see You in my eyes, when I open my heart as I talk to them.
Though difficulties arise, I know that in the diligent search of Your voice,
I can continue to get up and carry on.
It is so hard to keep a head held up high, Lord. When emails are piling, and employees feel entitled, I just want to coast my way through the day.
Wake me.
When I face the seemingly important people this week, remind me that You are far greater than any one of them.
Let me never compromise my obedience and love for the sake of a moment of glory for myself.
Instead, Father, let Your countenance radiate on my face
And let others see Your light through me.

Hide me in Your wings on this important week.
Visit me this week, my Jesus.
I yearn for Your presence.

In Your most precious name, I pray,
Amen

19 Or do you not know that your body is a temple of the Holy Spirit within you, whom you have from God? You are not your own,
20 for you were bought with a price. So glorify God in your body.
1 Corinthians 6:19-20

Week 4 Leadership Challenge:

How can you be more sensitive to the Lord's presence throughout this week?

Perseverance

Perseverance in holding on to the truth, no matter how we feel as leaders, is impossible especially if we do not have our True North. We look to scorecards, to Customer Experience surveys or even our own boss's compliments as our guide. The problem with that is they will fail us. They will not be faithful to their promises and will always depend on the tide. That is the nature of man.

Hold on to this prayer as a reminder that we do not have to rely on anything else but to the one Cornerstone who has sent us to be where we are.

Let us not grow weary of carrying our cross, for His yoke is easy, and His burden is far lighter than what the lies of the enemy brings (Matthew 11:30).

Praise you Father,

For I do not have to rely on my feelings
to know that You are with me.
Thank You that despite a seemingly screwed up day
the busyness of life, the noise on the streets,
and back to back to back meetings,
I am able to breathe out a sigh to You -
'all Yours, Lord!'
Let my purpose be only Yours.
Let this knowledge allow me to persevere
that my hands labor not in vain
because it is meant for Your glory.

Thank You that I can surrender this day to You
and through this prayer I can rest
on your command that I should not lean on my own
understanding but only trust You.
For if I acknowledge You in all my ways,
You will make my paths straight.

I carry my cross of leadership alongside with You
And I know that as I persevere, it is going to be so worth it.

I love your dearly, my Jesus,
Amen.

11 May you be strengthened with all power, according to his glorious might, for all endurance and patience with joy, 12 giving thanks[a] to the Father, who has qualified you[b] to share in the inheritance of the saints in light.
Colossians 1:11-12

Week 5 Leadership Challenge:

What are you willing to persevere in doing this week despite what others will say?

Letting Go

We might have heard from others that in order for our barns to be filled, or our cups to be poured into, we need to create a space for it. Many times, as a leader, we always yearn for more and more and we don't carefully think about what we need to let go.

Letting go is a crucial skill as much as taking in more. Sometimes, we assume that the Lord wants to bless us with more, but without properly tuning into His Word, we fail to hear His instructions of letting go – of the past, of grudges, of bitterness, or of activities that do not honor God. In my experience, I was able to fully live the life that He has called me to do by striving to cling on to His Word through reading of the Bible and diligent prayer for His grace.

Let this prayer allow us to reflect on things or people or activities that the Lord is asking us to Let go.

Dear Jesus,

Thank you for yet again, you have never failed me.
You woke me up, and gave me a brand new week.
Thank you for though with a very foolish heart that I carry, You still give me brand new mercies.
I come boldly in Your throne of Grace to worship You and seek for Your instructions.
Jesus please come and manifest Your vision for me this week.
Help me to see what steps I ought to take and not to take.
(take this time to pause and hear the whisper the leading of the Lord in your heart. Take your time, the Lord is in no rush)

Thank you for you will not lead me astray. Thank you for giving me the wisdom to know the importance of commitments and so I honor them by ensuring I do not over stretch myself. My commitment to You, to family, and to others reflect how much I desire to let others know who You are. And so may my decisions carefully be chosen to what will make your name glorified.

With Your grace, I say no to the works of the enemy this week, and I say YES to You.

Spirit fill me,
Amen

"Remember not the former things,
nor consider the things of old.
19 Behold, I am doing a new thing;
now it springs forth, do you not perceive it?
I will make a way in the wilderness
and rivers in the desert.
Isaiah 43:18-19

Meek 6 Leadership Challenge:

What have you been holding on to that you think the Lord is leading you to let go of?

Working with Excellence

Excellence, as we may have been taught, is not an inherited trait, nor something we learn in books. It is the product of doing a series of small things great so it becomes our habit. Many times, and especially when no one will notice, it is easy to be tempted to just ignore the dots on our "I's" and the cross on our "T's".

When we focus on our own image that comes from the affirmation of others and the zero's on our pay, we respond to it by focusing on what matters to them. The problem with that, however, is it results in an endless rat race, and a guaranteed failure. Man will always fail us (Romans 3:23), that is definite.

So what do we do? Do we then conclude that the workplace is an endless maze created by someone whose pleasure is to see the chasing of the tails? Do we then conclude that excellence is just a lucrative vice of this greater being who created this maze?

Without faith, it is impossible to please God (Hebrews 11:6). Our purpose ends up lukewarm and just getting by year after year. The Lord asks us to take our thoughts captive to whatever is excellent and worthy of praise. Then the Lord's peace will be with us (Philippians 4:8-9).

Heavenly Father,

We come to you with great need of your wisdom.
You are a good Father and you never cease to be faithful.
Let every intention of our hearts this week be everything that will bring glory to Your name.
Bless every work of our hands that produces excellence in small things and big things.
Let excellence be our habit so that others will see who our Father is.
Create delight in our hearts that we do not toil with grudge but with eagerness.
Help us remember that even Jesus, who is above all things, and in Him all things where created, had to work with wood as a carpenter every day until the right time of ministry came.
Let Your divine intervention create magnificence in all things that we do not for our own glory but for Yours.
And with your grace, as we strive to obey on all these things, may we never be tempted to touch Your glory.
May You be greater, and us lesser in all we do this week.

All honor and praise to Your name,

Amen

8 Finally, brothers, whatever is true, whatever is honorable, whatever is just, whatever is pure, whatever is lovely, whatever is commendable, if there is any excellence, if there is anything worthy of praise, think about these things. 9 What you have learned and received and heard and seen in me—practice these things, and the God of peace will be with you.
Philippians 4:8-9

Week 7 Leadership Challenge:

What will you do differently to show that you produce work with excellence?

When I fail

Failing is inevitable. No matter how good we think about who we are, we will definitely fail. Failing short of expectation, failing to connect more, to communicate enough. There will always be one reason or another to fail.

Some failures are easier to brush aside, than others. There are days when countless sleepless nights of preparation and hard work for you and your team leads to a completely disastrous meeting. Those days often bring us to a place where questions are asked – am I good enough? Is it worth it? Do I still want to do this?

We easily slip into an ugly place where we tend to forget who we are in Christ. We swing from being too proud to the other end of the spectrum, false humility. We second guess ourselves and replay the tape in our heads as to what went wrong.

God's child (John 1:12), Christ's friend (John 15:15), Bought by a price (1 Cor 6:20), Hidden with Christ in God (Colossians 3:3), Free from condemnation (Romans 8:1-2), Salt and Light (Matt 5:13), Can do all things through Christ (Philippines 4:13) – that is who we are.

Father, My Creator,

How great is Your persistent love, that no matter how many times I forget my identity in You, Your word comes alive and reminds me who I really am.
Let me not be the man who looks into the mirror and immediately forgets as he turns his back (James 1:24). Instead, with Your grace, let me rise up boldly in every failure and rejoice with gladness for the opportunity to experience Your Sovereignty.

You are the One who knit me in my mother's womb, and You know all the days ahead of me. You prepared the table in front of my enemies and sent your angels concerning me to lift me up so that I may never strike my foot against the stone.

Although it does feel like I have fallen really hard right now, and the pain does not feel like I'm by quiet waters, I fully trust that ALL things work together for my good because I love you.

I cast my sorrow to You, today. Every heartache, every failure, every guilt.
I nail at the foot of Your cross this (insert specific detail of failure).
Let Your words come alive and in my weakness be my strength right now.

Jehovah Nacham, come and hold me in Your arms and caress my aching soul.
Let Your will be done.
Let Your grace come down.
Let Your glory be exponentially more magnified with the failure I have and how You will turn it around.

In Jesus's name,

Amen.

9 But he said to me, "My grace is sufficient for you, for my power is made perfect in weakness." Therefore, I will boast all the more gladly of my weaknesses, so that the power of Christ may rest upon me. 10 For the sake of Christ, then, I am content with weaknesses, insults, hardships, persecutions, and calamities. For when I am weak, then I am strong.
2 Corinthians 12:9-11

Week 8 Leadership Challenge:

What have you failed in that you need to surrender to God? What do you think God is teaching you that you should work on this week?

New Beginnings

A new week brings excitement. It reminds me of the Lord's promise that His grace is new every morning. What a glorious gift to get a clean slate each day.

To some, new means great expectations – new team, new company, new job, or new promotion. It's a mixed emotion of anticipation, anxiety, and a bottled up energy that is ready to burst into making a difference.

To others, new means moving on, unprecedented change of having to do another thing without really choosing to do so. There are days when you just want things the way they were but it isn't. It is when new means rain when you're used to the sunshine.

Both chapters are experienced by every leader. It is that cyclical change that makes us better than before. That all we have with our people really are moments. Moments to cherish and intentionally lived, leaving a legacy that they can carry with them. Many times we ignore these moments, and in the end, we realize that we regret that we did.

Let this new beginning be purposeful. Let it spark new hopes, and dreams for people around us. God has gifted you the ability of leadership and may it be renewed today.

Oh Heavenly King,

I tremble in awe of your infinite love for me. I stand amazed by the golden rays of the sun peeking through the feathery clouds. How great and marvelous are your works.

As I plant my feet on the ground and breath in a new day, I want to remember that it is only by Your grace that I am standing again. Help me to be sensitive to your Holy Spirit prompting me of your love and instructions for this day.

Grant me new hopes, new dreams, and renewed joy in bringing honor and glory to Your name. As I face a new chapter in my leadership, may Your wisdom and knowledge guide me in reaching out to these people You have appointed to me.

I thank you for this opportunity to witness the work You have prepared before us. May all that we do bring honor and glory to Your name.

Take away every fear which is not coming from you. Turn my anxiety to trust and increased faith. You have chosen me to be here, and anointed me to proclaim of Your goodness. You will provide all that I need for You are ever with me.

As I begin a new chapter in my life, may Your word continue to be the light unto my feet that leads me to be the salt and light that You have called me to become.

I surrender to You this new page of my life to write the story You have planned for me.

I thank you, my Jesus.

In Your Precious Name,

Amen.

17 Therefore, if anyone is in Christ, the new creation has come: The old has gone, the new is here!
2 Corinthians 5:17

Week 9 Leadership Challenge:

How will you honor God this week on your new beginning?

Prayer before I Coach

Leadership is a great responsibility, as we all know. No matter how small or big our team is, the truth is, we are responsible for their lives. Not just lives of our direct reports, but lives of their families as well.

I have learned early in my career the difference between a leader and a manager. Many have written about this. We know what we should be aiming for is the former. There is no greater opportunity to be the leader that we aspire to be than by having a meaningful coaching conversation. This is when the rubber meets the road where the employee and the leader have that crucial discussion about performance and improvement.

This can be a life changing moment for our employees, or sometimes even for us. In the beginning, they may not be able to see, but then eventually, they can see because of guiding questions that lead them to realization. However, this will not come to pass without the persistent desire to penetrate them with a sincere heart.

Genuine love listens patiently.

Loving Jesus,

You have modeled to us the perfect way to be intimate with God.
At dawn, you awake and speak to Your Father before starting Your day.
I come before You now, with a surrendered heart to open my mouth so You can fill it with words as I speak to (name).

Send me Your Holy Spirit and fill me with Your wisdom that I may discern (name)'s true heart.
Allow me to be quick to listen, encourage, and uplift the spirit.
May I focus on productive ways of how we can both be accountable in improving areas that will lead to more success.

Grant me the discipline to follow through on our plans as Christ was patient in rebuking His disciples which sanctifies their souls.

Father, may I never focus on this conversation as a means to gain more fame, nor affirmation of how I am doing, rather, may this be about (name)'s abilities and areas of opportunities.

May I be focused on what he/she volunteers to commit to rather than imposing what I want.
Remind me if I am dominating the conversation rather than asking guiding questions and listening with my heart.

Rid us of all the whispers of the enemy and open our hearts with clear and sincere intentions.
May this coaching conversation be meaningful and life changing for both of us as it deepens our relationship.

Grant me the boldness to cite Your Word as the Holy Spirit prompts me.
Give both of us renewed perspective as we both delight in discovering new insights through our coaching conversation.

May everything that I say and do bring You glory, honor, and praise.

In Your most Powerful Name, I pray.

Amen

19 Know this, my beloved brothers: let every person be quick to hear,
slow to speak, slow to anger;
James 1:19

Week 10 Leadership Challenge:

How can you improve on your listening skills this week?

Inspiration

The Lord has made His majesty plain (Romans 1:19) for us to see. By looking at the magnificent clouds in the morning with glorious golden rays of sunlight utterly exposes His 1) identity, and 2) power.

Imagine that we are all created in His image and likeness. That we too have in us the ability to create the same inspiration to those around us.

Gone are the days where bosses tell and employees do. We now live in the age of inspirational leadership where as a leader, you draw others to buy into your vision so your people will have the same level of passion to thrive in obtaining your goals.

We may find ourselves inspired by our own bosses, or more than likely, not. However, we do not need to look for our boss, or even our parents, or anyone else to create that spark that will ignite a passion. Rather, we find it from the source of all light.

May this week bring us inspiration from sunrays and creation. In so doing, may we equally be an inspiration to others.

My glorious Creator,

From whom all creation was made, and all authority is given, Thank you for making it plain for me to see Your beauty and power.
I ask for your help this week to ignite flames in my heart and be the torch bearer that will pass on this fire of inspiration to all those that You have appointed around me.

Fan the flames in my heart and never let it die down.

When I speak, let your words overflow from my heart.
May it be arms from heavens that comforts those who mourn.

Grant me the Holy Spirit's wisdom and make it bridges that allows others who feel stuck pass through into the knowledge of truth.

May my actions set ablaze those who drag themselves to work unable to find their meaning and greater purpose.

I seek not of my own fame, but let me point to Your name. Because only through You, the sole source of light, I am able to even come to realize the power of inspiration.

I praise you endlessly.

Amen.

24 And you said, 'Behold, the Lord our God has shown us his glory and greatness, and we have heard his voice out of the midst of the fire. This day we have seen God speak with man, and man still live.
Deuteronomy 5:4

Week 11 Leadership Challenge:

How can you intentionally inspire others this week?

Thank You when my heart says, No Thank You.

What are we thankful for? It's easy to be thankful when life is good and worry seems does not to be visiting us for quite a while. However, when sickness strikes, or when unexpected expenses creep up, or even an overlooked detail causes a big loss in the business, the words praise or even rejoicing escapes our heart.

I'd like to think that the goodness of the Lord is as real as the sunlight. Like CS Lewis said, "I believe in Christianity as I believe that the sun has risen: not only because I see it, but because by it I see everything else." Would the sun cease to rise tomorrow because we are suffering today? I don't think so. The same is true with the glory and majesty of God. The same God who brought us to peaks, is the same God who is with us in valleys.

Jesus taught us how to pray when He walked on earth – "Our Father, who art in Heaven, Holy is Your Name." He did not say, holy is Your name today, because my bank account is balancing well. Jesus said, "Holy is Your name," period. I believe He meant, You are holy, always.

The famous Philippians 4:6 constantly reminds us that "with thanksgiving" we should be presenting our requests to God.

Gratitude is an attitude of faith and trust. It seeks our Father with great expectation saying, thank You for hearing me, thank You that despite my suffering, You remain faithful.

Oh Dear Jesus,

How I long that my heart is still rejoicing on Your great Name.
Many times in a day or even weeks, I ignore the value of the majesty You have painted in the sky. And I do not even deserve to see it.

I thank you for this day. I thank you for the joy that comes from the Holy Spirit's presence in my heart. The joy that is beyond money nor any other form of earthly security. But the sole joy of You and who You are in me.

I thank you for the sorrow, too. Though it is very hard to believe that this is going to work out for good, because I love you. Though it does not feel joyful or even close to peaceful right now, I thank you. Greater are you who is in me (1 John 4:4).

Grant me a grateful heart. When I see myself as pitiful, or even worthless, open my eyes to what is the treasure and inheritance that I have in You. I need You because I honestly find it very hard to find anything to be thankful for.

The refinement of anything valuable is through fire. Oh how precious Your thoughts are of me that You see me worth more than any precious stones. Though I only see the fire, and the seemingly eternal burn, Thank you.

It is only by Your grace, I am able to utter on wretched heart, Thank you.

With a surrendered heart, I pray,

Amen

4 Little children, you are from God and have overcome them, for he who is in you is greater than he who is in the world.
1 John 4:4

Week 12 Leadership Challenge:

What are you thankful for this week that is most difficult for you to be grateful about?

Humility

The most deceitful thing about leadership is the slow creeping pride that disguises itself as sacrifice. I remember dealing with the ugly face of self-esteem as I moved to the United States from the Philippines. I was in high spirits, as a new believer knowing with full conviction that I was brought by the Lord to this new territory to share the gospel to this foreign and dying land.

I was already in a position of influence in the Philippines and was dealing with Chief Executives. When I got to the US, what I expected did not come to pass. From managing hundreds of employees, I did not have direct reports, and when I did, felt like was treated like a Supervisor which is four levels lower than what I was in my home town. I kept asking God how he wants me to be the Salt and Light when He has not brought His appointed people for me to minister to. "Here I am Lord, use me!" I kept praying.

Until such time I realized when a dear friend of mine from the Philippines checked on me. I ranted about how unfulfilled I was because my boss at the time only knew about correcting my grammar on my presentations without appreciating the content. When I heard myself, I realized how bitter I had become and how I had become the opposite of becoming a witness for Christ.

It was so painful to realize that all along, I kept saying "I love you Jesus," and when the praise of my boss, or my peers, or my directs do not come back, my heart reveals what I really meant – "I love you, self."

Desire for self-esteem and selfishness is the root of pride and the pernicious lie that the enemy has planted in the world ever since the beginning of time (Genesis 3:1). May we, the mantle of humility, rest on us as we desire Jesus to be our deepest longing.

> 3 Do nothing from selfish ambition or conceit, but in humility count others more significant than yourselves.
> Philippians 2:3

Most Glorious King,

You hold both heaven and earth in Your mighty hand.
How magnificent is Your creation!

May Your name be lifted high and my name be so hidden in You.
It is my deepest desire for Your glory to increase, and I decrease (John 3:30).

While the enemy lures me using his old tactics of lust of the eyes and flesh,
Guard my heart from his snares and lead me to your quiet waters where I shall not be thirsty again.

Mold my heart and make it like yours.
Humble, compassionate, and generous.

Cast out all desires in my heart to please others but only desire the exaltation that comes from You (James 4:10).
Keep me hidden in my room as I pray to you in secret that only, You, my Father will know in secret and can reward me (Matthew 6:6).

Be my Potter, oh God and create Your masterpiece in me that I shall never boast of anything but of Your love.

Oh how loving and sweet are Your thoughts are for me. You have planned for me to excel for You even before the world began. You etched my name at the palm of Your hand and remembered me in Calvary.

To boast in this world is like a little kid boasting of that she has the sweetest candy, not realizing that she is heir to all of the world and the heavens! (Romans 4:13).

Make this truth be really real in my heart that I may stand on it and never be shaken by the lies of the enemy. No boss, nor CEO, nor presidents, or kings can separate me from Your love.

Make me humble that they may know who my Father is.

To Your Grace I implore,

Amen.

38 For I am sure that neither death nor life, nor angels nor rulers, nor things present nor things to come, nor powers, 39 nor height nor depth, nor anything else in all creation, will be able to separate us from the love of God in Christ Jesus our Lord.

Romans 8:38-39

Week 13 Leadership Challenge:

This week, who can you intentionally lift up and point credit to in public? How can you have less focus on yourself this week?

It is my prayer that this book has helped you in your leadership journey. If you have been touched in anyway and wanted to share your story, please feel free to send it directly to my email address at:

Chari.delacruz@gmail.com

May God's love and grace fill your heart.

www.ingramcontent.com/pod-product-compliance
Lightning Source LLC
Chambersburg PA
CBHW021414170526
45164CB00002B/639